MANY NATIONS

An Alphabet of Native America

by Joseph Bruchac

illustrated by Robert F. Goetzl

BridgeWater Paperback

For the generations to come
—J.B.

For my precious angels — Kim, Christopher, Elizabeth, and Joshua
—with love, R.G.

Text copyright © 1997 by Joseph Bruchac.

Illustrations copyright © 1997 by Robert F. Goetzl.

Published by BridgeWater Paperback, an imprint and trademark of Troll Communications L.L.C.

First published in hardcover by BridgeWater Books.

First paperback edition published 1998.

Designed by Dorit Radandt.

Printed in the United States of America.

10 9 8 7 6 5 4 3 2

Library of Congress Cataloging-in-Publication Data

Bruchac, Joseph, (date)

Many nations : an alphabet of Native America / by Joseph Bruchac ;

illustrated by Robert F. Goetzl.

p.   cm.

Summary: Illustrations and brief text present aspects of the lives of the many varied native peoples across North America.

ISBN 0-8167-4389-4 (lib. bdg.)   ISBN 0-8167-4460-2 (pbk.)

1. Indians of North America—Juvenile literature. 2. English language—Alphabet—Juvenile literature.
[1. Indians of North America—Miscellanea. 2. Alphabet.] I. Goetzl, Robert F., ill. II. Title.

E77.4.B78 1997

970' . 00497—dc21   97-12271

Anishinabe artists making birch bark bowls.

Blackfeet riders following buffalo herds.

Choctaw stickball players scoring goals.

Dakota children listening to the storyteller's words.

E Eagle circling high in the mountain air.

F Fox walking silent as the new day begins.

Goshute trackers moving like the bear.

Hopi grandfathers listening to the whispering winds.

Iroquois people planting a tree of peace.

Jemez Pueblo standing quiet as warm breezes blow.

Klallam carvers shaping canoes from the cedar trees.

Lummi women gathering clams when the tide is low.

Micmac hunters on the trail of the deer.

Navajo herders watching over their sheep.

Otoe fathers teaching sons how to walk with care.

Penobscot mothers singing little ones to sleep.

Quapaw villages along the stream.

Rappahannock nets moving with the tide.

Shinnecock dancers' feet shaping a dream.

Tuscarora farmers working side by side.

Umpqua grandmothers beading moccasins with pride.

V Visions of the future held in each child's eyes.

Wampanoag villages facing toward the dawn.

X marking the four directions from which we all come.

Yavapai people giving thanks for every sun.

Zuni elders saying prayers for the day that is done.

 Author's Note

One of the purposes of *Many Nations* is to help children recognize the diversity of Native Americans. Most readers are familiar with only a few of those nations, such as the Iroquois of the Northeast. More than four hundred different tribal nations were here before Columbus. And while the many cultures of Native Americans are very different, they all share traditions of respect for the natural world.

The text and illustrations in this book present a continent-wide cross section of Native American people relating to their environments. From the Northwest we see Klallam men (who wore mustaches long before Europeans came) making canoes from the great cedar trees and Lummi women gathering clams from Puget Sound.

In the Northeast we glimpse Micmac men wearing the hunting cap that resembles the head of a great horned owl; an old-style village of the Massachusetts Wampanoag, whose name means "People of First Light"; and contemporary Shinnecock dancers on Long Island dressed in Pan-Indian powwow regalia.

To the southeast we view Tuscarora farmers, Rappahannock people fishing the tidewaters, and Choctaw men engaging in a game that is a forerunner of modern lacrosse.

The Plains nations, where the introduction of the horse two centuries ago changed entire cultures, are represented by the Blackfeet, Otoe, and Dakota.

From the desert Southwest are the Yavapai of the Grand Canyon area; the people of Jemez Pueblo and Zuni, whose ancient villages have existed for many centuries; and the Navajo, who have built a new way of life around the herding of sheep within the last 150 years.

Those cultures portrayed in *Many Nations* are only a handful of the hundreds of surviving nations of Native America. It is my hope that this small book will encourage people to respect and learn more about the many original nations of our land.